CHANGING

CHINA

Dr Jen Green

W
FRANKLIN WATTS
LONDON • SYDNEY

First published in 2008 by Franklin Watts

© 2008 Arcturus Publishing Limited

Franklin Watts
338 Euston Road
London NW1 3BH

Franklin Watts Australia
Level 17/207 Kent Street, Sydney, NSW 2000

Produced by Arcturus Publishing Limited,
26/27 Bickels Yard, 151–153 Bermondsey Street, London SE1 3HA

The right of Jen Green to be identified as the author of this work has been asserted by her in accordance with the Copyright, Designs and Patents Act 1988.

Series concept: Alex Woolf
Editor and picture researcher: Cath Senker
Designer: Ian Winton
Illustrator: Stefan Chabluk

Picture credits:
Corbis: cover *left* (Keren Su), cover *right* (Bob Sacha), 14 (Bettmann), 15 (Peter Turnley), 18 (Reinhard Krause/Reuters), 20 (Michael Reynolds/epa/Corbis), 21 (Du Huaju/Xinhua Press), 34 (Bettmann), 40 (Liu Liqun), 41 (Keren Su).
EASI-Images (photos by Adrian Cooper unless otherwise stated): 6, 7 (Tony Binns), 10 (Tony Binns), 16, 19, 22, 23, 25, 26, 27, 28, 29, 31 (Tony Binns), 32 (Tony Binns), 37 (Rob Bowden), 38, 42, 43.
Photos.com: 33.
Shutterstock: 13 (Taolmor), 36 (Ke Wang).
Topfoto: 12 (Topham Picturepoint).

The illustrations on pages 9, 17 and 30 are by Stefan Chabluk.

Cover captions:
Left: A woman ploughs a field with a water buffalo.
Right: Evening shoppers in Shanghai.

Every attempt has been made to clear copyright. Should there be any inadvertent omission, please apply to the publisher for rectification.

A CIP catalogue record for this book is available from the British Library.

Dewey Decimal Classification Number: 915

ISBN 978 0 7496 8206 4

Printed in Malaysia

Franklin Watts is a division of Hachette Children's Books, an Hachette Livre UK company.
www.hachettelivre.co.uk

Contents

CHAPTER 1

Introduction

The People's Republic of China is one of the world's most rapidly changing nations. During the 20th century, the country passed through several major transformations. In 1900 China was an overwhelmingly rural nation with very little industry. It was ruled by an emperor and was largely cut off from the outside world. In 1911 imperial rule ended. Nearly four decades of war and unrest followed. In 1949 China became a Communist state – the second in the world after the Soviet Union (USSR). The government took control of the economy.

Between 1950 and the late 1970s, China modernized gradually and its economy grew slowly. Then from 1979, the government introduced sweeping economic reforms, which led to rapid modernization. Thousands of new businesses were launched. With astonishing speed,

Shanghai is China's largest city, with more than 13 million inhabitants. This photo shows one of the city's main highways lit up at night.

FOCUS: CHINA'S LARGEST CITIES

China has more than 100 cities with over a million inhabitants. Most cities are located along river valleys or coasts in the south and east. Beijing in the north-east is China's capital – a position it has held almost continuously since the 13th century. As well as the walled Forbidden City, former home of China's emperors, it has the main government buildings, ranged around the vast Tiananmen Square. Yet the largest city in China is not Beijing but the port of Shanghai, at the mouth of the Yangtze (Chang Jiang) River. In the past 20 years, Shanghai has seen huge changes that reflect China's economic transformation. Thousands of factories and businesses have opened here, and some of the world's tallest buildings have risen from a sprawl of building sites.

China's economy changed. Instead of the government controlling the economy, businesses could make their own decisions about producing, buying and selling goods and services.

Since the 1980s, China has become one of the world's largest economies. In turn, this has transformed many aspects of life in China, and posed challenges for the country's political leaders. China's economic transformation has not been matched by political transformation, and Communist rule remains in place.

Size and population

China is the world's fourth largest country after Russia, Canada and the United States (USA). A similar size to the United States, it has 1.3 billion people – over 20 per cent of the world's population. China's population is very unevenly distributed, with far more people living in the south and east than in the north and west. Most people still live in the countryside. However, this situation is changing quickly, as thousands of country dwellers move to the cities. There is a marked contrast between the fast pace of life in China's bustling modern cities and the slower pace in the countryside, where farming remains the dominant way of life.

Landscapes of China

Covering 9.6 billion square kilometres, China has many different landscapes, including mountains, plateaus (high, flat areas), tundra, plains, deserts and forests. Over half of this vast country is mountainous, with uplands (high land) rising to the Himalayas in the west.

Mount Everest, the world's highest peak at 8,850 m, lies on the border with Nepal. North of the Himalayas, the bleak Plateau of Tibet covers a quarter of China, with an average height of 4,000 m above sea level. Tibet has been part of China since 1950. North of the Plateau of Tibet lie vast tracts of windswept grasslands (open land covered in grass) and the Gobi and Takla Makan Deserts – two of the world's largest and coldest deserts.

From the western uplands, the land drops away towards the Pacific Ocean in the east. The eastern half of the country is mainly occupied by low-lying plains and the basins of mighty rivers. The Yangtze cuts through central-eastern China for 6,300 km. It is the world's third-longest river. To the north, the Yellow River (Huang He) has been farmed and settled for 5,000 years. These and other major rivers flood quite regularly. Over the

centuries they have covered the surrounding plains with fertile silt (sand and mud) that makes the land ideal for farming. China's plains and valleys are a patchwork of fields where farmers grow rice, wheat and other crops. However, floods along the Yangtze and Yellow Rivers have also killed thousands of people.

Climate

Spanning 30 degrees of latitude from north to south, China has a wide variety of climates, ranging from subarctic (very cold) in the north to temperate (mild) in the central-eastern area, and subtropical (warm) in the far south-east. Altitude – height above sea level – also has a major influence on climate. The Himalayas and the Plateau of Tibet experience long, bitterly cold winters and brief summers. The Yangtze is often said to divide the country into two broad climate zones. South of the river, frosts are rare and rainfall is generally plentiful, while north of the Yangtze, the climate is generally cold and often dry.

COMPARING COUNTRIES: CHINA AND THE USA BASIC FACTS

	China	United States
Total area	9,596,960 sq km	9,826,630 sq km
World ranking in size	4	3
Coastline	14,500 km	19,924 km
Highest point	Mt Everest: 8,850 m	Mt McKinley: 6,194 m
Longest river	Yangtze	Mississippi
Capital	Beijing	Washington, DC
Population size *	1,321,851,890	301,139,947
Largest city	Shanghai	New York
Form of government	Communist state	democracy

* 2007 estimates

Source: CIA Factbook, 2008

Southern and eastern parts of China are affected by monsoon winds, which change direction with the seasons and bring rain at certain times of year. In winter, winds blowing off the Asian mainland bring dry weather. In summer, winds blowing off the Indian and Pacific Oceans bring heavy rain. The deserts of the north and west receive less than 25 cm of rain annually. In the same region, the Turpan Pendi (Tulufan Depression) is the hottest part of China, with temperatures soaring to 48° C in summer. This is also China's lowest point, 154 m below sea level.

Key
- ■ Capital city
- ● Other cities
- ⋖⋖⋖ Great Wall of China
- ▲ Mountain

RUSSIA

KAZAKHSTAN

Altai Mountains

MONGOLIA

Gobi Desert

Xiao Hinggan Range

Huzhong Nature Reserve

Hanma Nature Reserve

Da Hinggan Range

Manchurian Plain

M a n c h u r i a

● Harbin

Changbai Nature Reserve

KYRGYZSTAN

Tian Shan

Turpan Pendi

XINJIANG

Takla Makan Desert

Tarim Basin

Kunlun Mountains

Qaidam Basin

INNER MONGOLIA

Mu us Desert

Loess Plateau

NINGXIA

HuangHean River (Yellow River)

● Shenyang

NORTH KOREA

Dalian

SOUTH KOREA

SEA OF JAPAN

JAPAN

Beijing ■ *TIANJIN*

YELLOW SEA

C H I N A

Xi'an ●

Qin Mountains

SHAANXI

Baishui River Nature Reserve

Mekong River

Salween River

Chang Jiang River (Yangtze River)

Nanjing ●

● Shanghai

Wuhan ●

HUBEI

EAST CHINA SEA

Plateau of Tibet

TIBET

Wenchuan Wolong Nature Reserve

SICHUAN

Chongqing ●

Sichuan Basin

FUJIAN

Himalayas

NEPAL

▲
Mount Everest 8,850 m

BHUTAN

Himalayas

BANGLADESH

INDIA

N

GUANGXI

Nan Mountains

Kunming ●

GUANGDONG

Guanzhou ● ● Shenzhen

Hong Kong

Macao

TAIWAN

0   miles   500

0   kilometres   500

MYANMAR (BURMA)

BAY OF BENGAL

LAOS

VIETNAM

THAILAND

Hainan

PHILIPPINES

China is the largest country in Asia. This map of China shows the main geographical features and places mentioned in this book. It includes an inset showing the country's location in eastern Asia.

CHAPTER 2

History

China is an ancient country, with a history stretching back 5,000 years. Around 3,000 BCE, civilization began along the banks of the Yellow River. People started farming and later making pottery and working metals such as iron. Around 1,700 BCE, the Chinese started to develop a form of writing.

China becomes an empire

In ancient times, China was a patchwork of small kingdoms, but in 221 BCE a warrior-prince named Ying Zheng defeated his rivals to become Qin Shi Huangdi, China's first emperor. He founded the first dynasty (ruling family), the Qin (pronounced Chin), after which China is thought to have been named. He also began to build a Great Wall to keep out northern invaders, a huge project that was eventually completed by later rulers.

The empire founded by Qin Shi Huangdi survived for 2,000 years, although other dynasties, some of them foreign, replaced the Qin. The reign of a strong dynasty was

The Great Wall of China is the world's largest human-made structure, stretching for some 6,700 km. Although much of it has crumbled into ruins, it is still a remarkable structure, and a major tourist attraction.

CHINA'S DYNASTIES

China's history is divided into dynasties – periods of rule by powerful families. Each new dynasty brought fresh achievements in art and science or the expansion of China's empire.

Year	Dynasty	Achievements
1766–1122 BCE	Shang dynasty	Oldest written records
1122–221 BCE	Zhou dynasty	Time of the philosopher Confucius
221–207 BCE	Qin dynasty	First Chinese empire
206 BCE–220 BCE	Han dynasty	Effective rule develops; arts and science thrive

Year	Dynasty	Achievements
220–581 CE	Intermediate period	China is split into three kingdoms
581–618	Sui dynasty	China is unified again
618–907	Tang dynasty	Arts flourish

Year	Dynasty	Achievements
907–960	Second intermediate period	
960–1279	Song dynasty	Civil service develops
1279–1368	Yuan dynasty	Reign of Mongol rulers
1368–1644	Ming dynasty	Mongols are pushed out; literature and art flourish
1644–1911	Ch'ing dynasty	Emperors from Manchuria are China's last dynasty

usually a time of peace and prosperity. These eras were interspersed with periods of unrest between dynasties. As the Han, Tang and Song dynasties succeeded the Qin, so China gradually expanded its borders, and an increasingly efficient civil service was established to run the huge country.

Early achievements

Arts, science and medicine flourished during times of peace in China. Throughout the early Christian age and medieval period in Europe, China led the world in astronomy, mathematics and science, and built fine cities. The Chinese had invented silk, paper and printing by 500 CE. Inventions such as the compass, crossbow, wheelbarrow and gunpowder were used in China centuries before they appeared in the West.

The Ch'ing dynasty

In 1644 the Ming dynasty that had ruled China since the 1360s was replaced by the Ch'ing from Manchuria, in the north-east. At first the Ch'ing were strong rulers, but by the late 18th century their power had weakened. European powers such as Britain and France saw a chance to gain influence and develop trade links with China.

Chinese goods such as silk, porcelain (fine pottery) and tea were highly valued in Europe, but the Chinese had little interest in European goods. During the early 19th century, the British sought to balance their imports from China by exporting the drug opium. China tried to ban the import of opium, which led to two wars with Britain, in 1839–42 and 1858–60. Britain won both conflicts, gaining a valuable territory – the island of Hong Kong. In the late 19th century, China was forced to make similar agreements with other European powers. Britain, France and Germany established separate 'spheres of interest' within China, where they behaved like colonial rulers.

China becomes a republic

By 1900 there was growing dissatisfaction with Ch'ing rule among ordinary Chinese people. A revolutionary nationalist movement aimed at

During the early twentieth century, there was increasing hostility to imperial rule among ordinary Chinese. This photo, taken in 1911, shows a large gathering of revolutionaries in Peking (now Beijing).

toppling the emperor gathered strength. In 1911 revolutionaries led by a teacher, Sun Yat-sen, deposed the last emperor, ending 2,000 years of imperial rule. The revolutionaries, now called the Kuomintang, or National Party, proclaimed the Chinese Republic in 1912. However, the Nationalists were unable to gain control over all of China. Almost immediately, fighting broke out between warlords – independent military leaders in different regions who were each trying to extend their power.

Civil war

By 1922 there was full-scale civil war between the Kuomintang, now under the leadership of Chiang

CASE STUDY: MAO ZEDONG (1893–1976)

Mao Zedong was one of the most influential figures of the 1900s. Born into a wealthy farming family, he became a Communist while working as a librarian at Beijing University. Mao assumed leadership of the Communist forces during the Long March (1934–5). He believed that revolution was an ongoing process, but some of his schemes caused great hardship in China.

The Communists finally triumphed over the Nationalists in 1949, and Mao proclaimed the People's Republic of China in Beijing. The Nationalists fled to the island of Taiwan off south-east China, where they set up a rival government, the Republic of China.

A policeman stands to attention under a large portrait of Chairman Mao that hangs above the entrance to Tiananmen Gate in Tiananmen Square. The former leader's mausoleum (tomb) lies nearby.

Kai-Shek, and the warlords. For a time the Kuomintang formed an alliance with a new force, the Communists, in an effort to unite China. The Chinese Communist Party (CCP) had been founded in 1921, inspired by the triumph of Communism in Russia in 1917. Then in 1927, fighting broke out between the former allies.

By 1934 the Kuomintang had isolated a Communist army led by a scholar named Mao Zedong in the south-east. Mao ordered a tactical retreat, marching his troops west and then north to join other Communist forces in Shaanxi. Hundreds of thousands died in what became known as the Long March, but Mao emerged as leader of the Chinese Communists.

Triumph of Communism

During World War II, both Communists and Nationalists fought against Japan, which had invaded China in 1937. Fighting between the two parties resumed following Japan's surrender in 1945.

Mao now set out to rebuild China, devastated by decades of war, in accordance with Communist principles. Faced with the enormous task of providing for a huge population, all farms and factories were taken under state control. Citizens were organized into work units called *danweis*. The government controlled every aspect of life, including the allocation of work and housing, and there was little personal freedom. In return, Mao promised the 'iron rice bowl' – guaranteed food, work, housing, schooling and healthcare for all citizens.

FOCUS: THE CULTURAL REVOLUTION

In 1966 Mao announced a new policy called the Great Proletarian Cultural Revolution. The aim was to put China back on the path of true revolution by stopping reform within the Communist Party and stamping out traditional values and beliefs. Young people, particularly students, became Mao's 'Red Guard'. They were encouraged to denounce intellectuals and reformers, even among senior Party members. Anyone accused of not being revolutionary enough could be publicly humiliated, beaten up or worse. They might be sent for 're-education' in a forced labour camp or even executed. Chaos reigned as schools and universities were shut, and China lost part of its priceless ancient heritage as temples and books were destroyed. Finally in 1968, Mao disbanded the Red Guards and restored order.

Young people perform a song and mime criticizing the philosopher Confucius during the Cultural Revolution. The ideas of this ancient Chinese thinker were condemned at the time.

The Great Leap Forward

During the 1950s, China modernized with the help of its ally, the Soviet Union. Economic growth was slow. There was barely enough food, and many industries were inefficient (badly run). In 1958 Mao announced an efficiency drive called the Great Leap Forward. Ambitious targets were set for increasing food and steel production. The scheme was poorly planned and managed. By 1961 it had resulted in a countrywide famine (severe shortage of food) and millions died. Mao resigned as chairman of the CCP. However, he regained control of the party by the mid-1960s.

A new order

Mao died in 1976. A struggle for power between old-style Communists, or 'conservatives', and reformers followed. By 1978 a reformer named Deng Xiaoping had gained control. Deng's vision was different from Mao's. He immediately began a

Chinese students demonstrated in Tiananmen Square in 1989, calling for increased democracy. Many young people were killed or arrested when the government suppressed the protest in July.

programme of sweeping economic reform called the 'Four Modernizations', which allowed people to establish their own businesses.

By the late 1980s, many Chinese people were hoping for political reform to match the economic changes of the decade. In 1989 thousands of students gathered to protest for democratic reform in front of the government buildings in Tiananmen Square, Beijing. After six weeks, the government ordered troops to break up the demonstrations. The soldiers opened fire on a crowd of unarmed protesters. Hundreds were killed and many more were arrested. Personal freedom is still limited in China, which has a poor record on human rights (see Chapter 4).

CHAPTER 3

Economic Change

China is one of the world's fastest-growing economies. In 2000 it ranked fifth in the world in terms of Gross Domestic Product (GDP) – the total value of goods and services produced in a year. In 2006 that ranking had risen to second, after the United States, and experts predict it will soon become the world's largest economy. China's high ranking is partly due to its huge population. Yet because of its population size, it ranks much lower in terms of GDP per person – far below the United States, Japan and other leading economies.

China's economic strengths include plentiful natural resources as well as a large workforce.

For much of its history, until the late 1970s, China had little interest in trade with the outside world. Its new-found wealth is based on manufacturing and exports.

Opening up to trade

In 1978 Deng Xiaoping signalled his willingness to trade with the West by announcing an 'Open Door' policy. In 1979 he introduced sweeping economic reforms within China that allowed people to set up their own companies. Almost immediately, tens of thousands of new companies began to open their doors for business. At the same time, inefficient state-owned industries were either closed or sold off to private companies

Pudong District in Shanghai was one of the areas opened to foreign business in the 1980s. These modern high-rise buildings reflect the city's new-found wealth.

COMPARING COUNTRIES: THE CHINESE AND THE JAPANESE ECONOMIES

China's economy is growing faster than Japan's, but on average, the Chinese people are far poorer than the Japanese.

GDP in China and Japan	China	Japan
GDP*	$10.21 trillion	$4.218 trillion
GDP real growth rate*	11.1%	2.2%
GDP per capita *	$7,800	$33,100

* estimated figures 2006

Source: CIA Factbook

(owned by individuals). Agriculture changed too; farms were no longer run by the government.

Deng's new policies included the setting up of five Special Economic Zones (SEZs) in the south and east: in Shenzhen, Zhuhai and Shantou in Guangdong, Xiamen in Fujian, and on Hainan Island. In order to encourage foreign businesses to invest in the SEZs, the government allowed them to pay low taxes. In the 1980s, the open zone was extended to include more coastal areas, including Pudong District in Shanghai. In the 1990s, further major cities opened to foreign trade.

Deng's 'Open Door' policy was designed to boost the country's economy and bring in new technology. In the space of just 25 years, China transformed its economy from a state-controlled system into one in which businesses were free to produce and sell their goods. Nevertheless, the government has kept some control over the economy, running certain key businesses and controlling the prices of some products and services. It also controls most banking and foreign trade. Overall, China's economic policy has proved remarkably successful. The economy has expanded tenfold since 1980, and is still growing by an extraordinary 9–10 per cent each year.

China's labour force by occupation, 2005

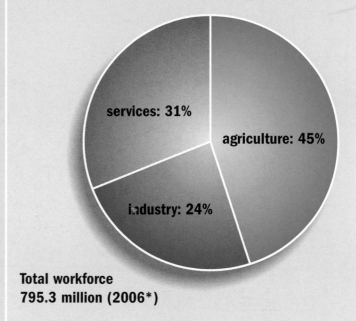

services: 31%

agriculture: 45%

industry: 24%

Total workforce 795.3 million (2006*)

* estimated figure
Source: CIA World Factbook, 2008

Japan's labour force by occupation, 2004

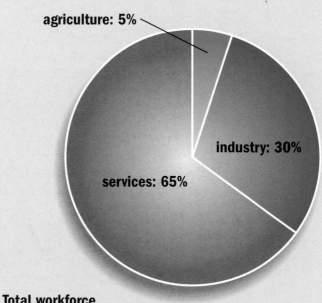

agriculture: 5%

industry: 30%

services: 65%

Total workforce 66.57 million (2006*)

* estimated figure
Source: CIA World Factbook, 2008

Industry and manufacturing

China's economy can be divided into three main sectors: agriculture, services and manufacturing (including mining). Manufacturing is the most important sector, providing around half of the country's GDP. Shanghai is by far the biggest industrial centre, followed by Beijing, Tianjin, Wuhan, Xi'an and coastal cities such as Shenyang, Guangzhou and Kunming.

In the 1950–1970s, heavy industry such as shipbuilding and steel-making were extremely important. The country is still a leading producer of steel, vehicles such as ships, tractors, trucks, machinery, and also cement and fertilizers. However, the last 20 years have seen a shift to light industry – the production of goods such as toys, clothing, footwear and electronic goods. Televisions, DVD players and mobile phones are manufactured both for export and also for a growing number of Chinese consumers. As average earnings in China have risen, the

A worker assembles electronic parts in a television factory in Guangdong. Low labour costs enable China to produce goods such as televisions more cheaply than in the West.

market for goods within the country has become increasingly important.

Agriculture

Traditionally, agriculture was the basis of China's economy. For the government, feeding the country's huge population is still top priority, but the percentage that agriculture contributes to GDP is declining. It was less than 12 per cent in 2006.

Less than 15 per cent of China is suitable for farming, because huge areas are occupied by mountains, deserts and other land where nothing grows. In the south, the most important crops include rice, cotton, tea and sweet potatoes, while in the north, wheat, millet and sorghum (types of grain) are grown. Farmers also grow a huge variety of fruits and vegetables, and raise livestock such as chickens, ducks and pigs.

The farming sector includes fishing and forestry. China's fishing industry is one of the world's largest, with fish farming (breeding fish) playing an important role. The country's largest forests lie in the north-east and in Sichuan and Tibet in the west. In recent years, deforestation has caused environmental problems (see Chapter 7).

Services

The service sector includes banking, trade, education, health, communication and transport. In 2006 this fast-growing sector of the economy employed around one-third of all workers and provided around 40 per cent of GDP. Tourism is a major growth industry within the service sector.

FOCUS: WATER RESOURCES

Water is scarce in many parts of China, despite having two of the world's largest rivers, the Yangtze and Yellow Rivers. Beijing, Tianjin and 400 other cities experience water shortages for much or part of the year. The south generally has enough water, but the north is much drier. To solve this problem, a massive engineering project is underway to transport water from south to north. The South-to-North Water Transfer Project involves the construction of three major canals across the country. Begun in 2002, it is scheduled for completion around 2050, at a projected cost of almost US $60 billion.

A farm worker plants out rice seedlings. Since 1950, the percentage of the workforce engaged in farming has fallen steadily, from 78 per cent in 1970 to less than half of all workers today.

Working conditions

An important reason for China's economic growth is that it has low wage rates compared to the West. Because Chinese workers earn lower wages, goods can be produced more cheaply. Working conditions are generally worse than in Western countries. Some companies force their workers to work long hours. Workers' rights are limited and it is illegal to go on strike.

Natural resources – minerals and energy

China's economic success is partly based on its rich natural resources, including minerals and energy. The country is a leading producer of iron ore, magnesium, tin and tungsten (used to make steel and light bulbs). It also has large stocks of aluminium, copper, lead, gold, silver, zinc, titanium and many other minerals. The most important mining areas are the centre and the north-east.

China is one of the world's top coal-producing nations, ranking third after the United States and Russia. The largest coalfields lie in the north, from where coal must be transported right across China to industrial zones in the south and east. China also has huge reserves of oil and natural gas. The largest oilfield is Daqing in the north-east, while the Tarim Basin in the west is the most important gas-producing region.

Two mine workers carry a load of coal at a small mine in China. Coal supplies over 70 per cent of China's energy, but at great cost to the environment. Also, many workers die in mining accidents each year.

CASE STUDY: THE THREE GORGES DAM

The Three Gorges Dam on the Yangtze River in Hubei Province is the world's largest dam, rising 185 m high and stretching 2 km across the river. Located on a scenic stretch where the Yangtze passes through sheer gorges, it has been built to provide hydroelectricity, water for irrigation and also to control flooding. The project attracted criticism because it involved creating a 650-km reservoir (man-made lake) behind the dam. Several major cities, with a total population of 1.2 million, had to be moved to make way for the rising water. Construction of the dam began in 1993 and it will be fully working in 2011. When this happens, it is expected to provide 10 per cent of China's energy needs.

Energy use

Energy use is rising incredibly fast with the expansion of industry and manufacturing in China. Domestic energy use has also risen steeply because the living standards of many people have improved. Energy use per person doubled in the 25 years between 1980 and 2004, and looks set to double again by 2015.

Around three-quarters of China's energy comes from coal-burning power stations. China is one of the world's leading consumers as well as producers of coal. Its use of coal increased five-fold between 1970 and the mid-1990s. In addition, it is the world's second-largest consumer of oil after the United States.

The Three Gorges Dam cost US $25 billion to build. The reservoir that formed behind the dam flooded 27,900 hectares of land.

In 2005 China produced 3.6 million barrels of oil per day, which supplied just over half of its needs of 6.5 million barrels daily. It has to import the rest, mainly from the Middle East and Russia. China's use of fossil fuels causes serious pollution (see Chapter 7).

China currently obtains about one-fifth of its energy from renewable sources such as hydroelectricity. Dams have been built on many swift-flowing rivers to channel water past turbines that work generators. China has 22,000 dams more than 17 m high. The country's largest and best-known hydroelectric scheme is the Three Gorges Dam Project (see page 21). The nation currently has three nuclear power plants, and there are plans to build more.

Transport

For centuries, China's development was hampered by its poor transport system. In the 1990s, it began a massive programme to improve its

Bicycles are traditionally the main form of transport in China. In recent years, the number of cars on the roads has risen steeply, causing an increase in traffic and air pollution.

transport links including roads, railways, airports and waterways (rivers and canals).

Railways are the most important mode of transport in China, and the main means of travelling long distances. The rail network is largely run and funded by the state. It includes some fast inter-city routes, such as between Nanjing and Shanghai. More high-speed routes are planned to link cities such as Beijing, Harbin and Guangzhou. Four cities – Beijing, Shanghai, Tianjin and Guangzhou – have underground rail networks.

China's 1.87 million kilometres of roads include 34,000 km of motorways. Again, some major inter-city routes are under construction. In the

TRANSPORT

Railway tracks: 75,438 km

Roads: 1,870,661 km, including paved 1,515,797 km; unpaved 354,864 km

Number of cars per 1,000 people: 8 (2003)

Airports with paved runways: 403

Airports with unpaved runways: 64

Waterways: 124,000 km usable by boats (2006)

Largest ports: Dalian, Guangzhou, Ningbo, Qingdao, Qinhuangdao, Shanghai, Shenzhen, Tianjin

Sources: CIA Factbook and World Resources Institute, 2008

countryside though, many roads are not even paved. The bicycle is the traditional mode of transport along China's roads; in rural areas, carts are pulled by oxen and donkeys. There are still some 300 million bicycles, but car use is increasing rapidly – from 1 million cars in 1990 to 10 million by 2003. People also travel using buses and motorcycles, with rickshaws (carts pulled by bicycles) and taxis used in towns.

Air travel is growing rapidly for transporting passengers and also goods, including raw materials and manufactured goods. Besides the main international airports of Beijing, Guangzhou, Hong Kong and Shanghai, there are more than 400 smaller airports.

Sea and freshwater transport is important in China. Major seaports include Dalian, Guangzhou, Hong Kong and Shanghai. China has thousands of kilometres of inland waterways, vital for transporting bulky goods such as grain and minerals. As well as major rivers, there is also an extensive network of canals, which includes the Grand Canal. This runs for more than 1,800 km, linking the Yangtze and Yellow Rivers. Work is underway to deepen the Grand Canal to allow passage by large ships.

Passengers disembark from a plane that has just landed at Beijing Airport. Only well-off Chinese can afford to travel by plane.

CHAPTER 4

Social Changes

The triumph of Communism in 1949 produced sudden and radical change within Chinese society. Since the 1980s, China's economic boom has also transformed society in a slightly more gradual but no less dramatic way.

Country and city

For much of the 20th century, China's population was overwhelmingly rural. In 1970 just 20 per cent of people lived in cities. Recent decades have seen large-scale migration to urban areas. By 2005, 43 per cent of the population were city-dwellers. Chinese society is expected to be mostly urban by 2015.

People leave the countryside to seek better-paid work and wider opportunities in towns. Wages in rural areas are low – about one-third of the average wage in cities. Country areas also have lower living standards, with many families unable to afford a refrigerator or motorcycle, let alone a TV, tractor or car. In some remote areas, villages lack electricity and sanitation (safe washing and toilet facilities).

In contrast, city life offers the chance of higher living standards. Most urban families have a refrigerator and TV, and some have cars and computers too. Yet since the 1980s, mass migration to the cities has created cramped conditions there. Many families rent one or two rooms in an apartment block, whereas in rural areas, many homes have six rooms. In both the countryside and cities, it is still common to find grandparents, parents and children living together.

CHINA'S POPULATION

Population: 1,321,851,890 (July 2007 estimate)

Population distribution:
urban: 43 per cent
rural: 57 per cent (2005)

Age structure
0–14: 20.4%
15–64: 71.7%
65 and over: 7.9%

Population growth rate: 0.6% per year (2007 estimate)

Life expectancy:
males: 71.1 years
females: 74.8 years

Fertility rate (average number of children women have):
1.75 children per woman

Population of largest cities (in millions):
Shanghai: 13.46
Beijing: 9.88
Guangzhou: 7.55
Wuhan: 6.79
Tianjin: 6.76
Shenzhen: 6.48
Chongqing: 6.17

Source: CIA Factbook and World Book Encyclopedia, 2008

In the early days of Communism, everyone was placed in a work unit, and people were rarely permitted to move to another part of China. Now the old-style work units have been abandoned, and restrictions on migration have partly been lifted. Young men arrive from the countryside to work on building sites in cities. Young women move to the open cities (cities open to trade with the West) to work in electronics factories. They often live in dormitory accommodation provided by their employers and work long hours in order to send money home.

China's economic success has certainly led to increased job opportunities and higher wages, but there are also problems. Unemployment has risen now that jobs are no longer secure. A new middle-class of wealthy, well-educated

Pedestrians cross a road in downtown Shanghai. The city's skyline has been transformed over the past 20 years, with high-rise buildings replacing older, low-rise housing.

businesspeople has emerged, with a growing gulf between these city folk and the unskilled poor.

Health

The gulf between rich and poor is having a growing effect on the health of the population. China provides basic health care for everyone, but people who can afford it may pay for better care. Chinese people live to about 72 on average. This figure is much higher than it was in the 1960s, when most people only lived to about 40. As well as Western medicine, traditional Chinese medicine is still practised, including herbal medicine, massage and acupuncture.

破除早婚陋习
提倡晚婚晚育

中共从江县委员会
从江县人民政府

Family size

The family has always been central to Chinese society. Large families were traditionally the norm. Around 1900 it was common for parents to have four or five children, who would look after them in old age. In the 1950s and 1960s, China's population grew rapidly. The government feared the rising population would soon threaten its ability to feed and provide for all its citizens. In 1979 it introduced a programme called the One-Child Policy. Married couples had to gain official approval to have a child, and faced heavy fines if they gave birth to a second one.

The One-Child Policy succeeded in limiting population growth, but it also produced lasting social change. Particularly in rural areas, couples preferred to have a son as their only child, to carry on the work of farming. Thousands of baby girls were aborted before birth (the pregnancy was

This family planning poster aims to encourage Chinese couples to value girl children. The photo was taken in an ethnic minority village in south-eastern China.

deliberately ended) or were abandoned to be brought up in orphanages. This led to a gender imbalance in Chinese society, with males outnumbering females by more than ten to one in some areas. It also led to a culture of spoiling only sons, who were nicknamed 'little emperors'.

The One-Child Policy has now been somewhat relaxed. People from ethnic minorities and rural areas are allowed to have more than one child. Family sizes are still small in China, partly because it is expensive to bring up children. There are still restrictions on families – it is illegal for men under the age of 22 to marry, and for women under 20. Most couples wait until their late twenties to have one or two children.

Education

The Chinese government is proud of its record of providing education for its citizens. All children between the ages of 6 and 16 are supposed to attend school. However, many children leave after completing their primary education. In poor families, children often have to work to boost the family income, and parents cannot afford the secondary school fees.

Children reading at their desks at a primary school. These pupils are from China's Miao community – an ethnic minority group from the south. Primary education is free in China, but parents have to pay for their children to attend secondary school.

FOCUS: ETHNIC MINORITIES IN CHINA

The majority of people in China – 92 per cent (2005) – are Han Chinese in origin. This name dates back to the days of the Han Empire, based in eastern-central China. There are also some 55 ethnic minority groups, each with their own language, culture and sometimes, religious beliefs. Most of these live near China's land borders and in the west and far south. Among the largest groups are the Zhuang of Guangxi in the south, the Hui of northern and central China, who are Muslims, and the Uygurs of the north-west. There are also large numbers of Tibetans, Kazakhs and Mongols.

A statue of the Chinese philosopher Confucius inside the Confucian Temple complex of Kong Miao, in Qufu, the town of his birth. Confucius stressed the importance of respect within the family and in society in general. He taught that children had a duty to obey their parents, and that people should obey their rulers.

In China, pupils are expected to work hard. The school day lasts from around 7 am to 4 or 5 pm. After school, even young children have to do several hours' homework. Class sizes are generally large, with up to 60 pupils in some areas. Apart from science, maths and history, primary-school children start to learn the Chinese script, which is based on thousands of symbols called characters. The official language, putonghua (Mandarin) is written the same way throughout China, but pronunciation varies greatly, with at least five major regional variations.

Only about half of all of pupils finish their secondary education, and a mere 2 per cent continue on to higher education. Competition for places at colleges and universities is fierce, since there are a tiny number of places compared

FOCUS: RELIGION

China has no official religion. During the Cultural Revolution, religion was strongly discouraged, and many temples and churches were torn down. Now people are freer to practise a religion if they choose. Buddhism has the widest following. It began in India and reached China in about 100 CE. Confucianism and Taoism are two ancient Chinese faiths. Confucianism is based on the teachings of Confucius, who lived around 500 BCE, while the mystic religion of Taoism was founded around the same time by the philosopher Laozi. About 2 per cent of Chinese are Muslims, and about 3 per cent are Christians.

to the huge number of bright, able pupils who complete secondary education.

Leisure time

Officially, the Chinese people now have more leisure time than during the early days of Communism. In the 1990s, the government introduced the two-day weekend. Yet many people still work six days a week. In 1998, week-long breaks were added to three traditional one-day holidays: the Chinese New Year in January or February, Labour Day on May 1, and National Day on October 1.

Many leisure activities take place out of doors since space is cramped in Chinese houses. People play pool or table tennis on the streets, or go to parks to fly kites. Older people meet in tea houses to play cards or the board game mahjong. Cities have a wide range of leisure activities, such as cinemas, theatres, karaoke bars and nightclubs. People visit the new shopping malls or meet at Western-style fast food outlets.

The Chinese are passionate about sport. Table tennis, badminton, basketball, volleyball, football, snooker, golf and gymnastics are all highly popular in China. Traditional martial arts, which began in China 3,000 years ago, have a big following. These include karate, kung fu and tai-chi. The general enthusiasm for sport was boosted when it was announced in 2001 that the 2008 Olympic Games would be held in Beijing.

After school, many Chinese children go to district sports schools like this one to practise their favourite sport. Table tennis is very popular in China.

CHAPTER 5

Political Changes

The economic changes that have transformed China since the 1980s were set in motion by a major shift in thinking on the part of the country's political leaders. Yet the political system itself remains largely unchanged. The CCP, which took power in 1949, is still in office.

China's constitution defines its government as a 'democratic dictatorship'. This is true in the sense that China is ruled by a government placed in power by the people. However, in practice the government has absolute power. The CCP is the overwhelmingly dominant political party, although small parties strongly influenced by the CCP are permitted. Communist Party members hold all the most powerful positions in the government and the legal system.

China's government is based in Beijing. The main decision-making body is the Politburo, made up of about 25 high-ranking CCP officials. The head of the Party is the General Secretary, who is also China's president. When Deng Xiaoping died in 1997, another reformer, Jiang Zemin, succeeded him as president. Hu Jintao became president in 2003. The prime minister is head of government. Wen Jaibao became prime minister in 2003.

There is another government body called the National Party Congress. It is made up of about 2,100 officials selected by CCP members all over China, but holds little real power. It meets for only a few weeks each year to approve the laws and policies of the Politburo.

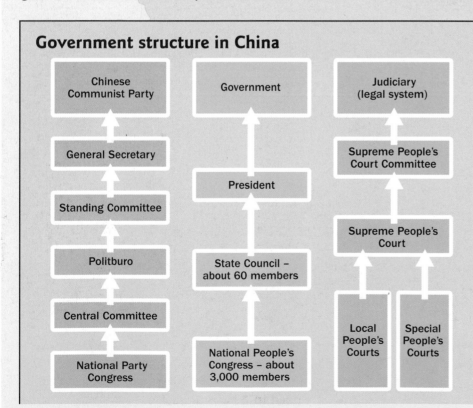

Government structure in China

- Chinese Communist Party
- General Secretary
- Standing Committee
- Politburo
- Central Committee
- National Party Congress

- Government
- President
- State Council – about 60 members
- National People's Congress – about 3,000 members

- Judiciary (legal system)
- Supreme People's Court Committee
- Supreme People's Court
- Local People's Courts
- Special People's Courts

This diagram shows the structure of the Chinese government and the judiciary.

The CCP is the largest political organization in the world. About 5 per cent of China's population are members. Since 2002, business owners have been allowed to join the Party – an important change, reflecting the government's acknowledgement of the growing influence of private companies.

Provinces of China

The People's Republic of China is made up of 33 divisions, including 22 provinces and four municipalities (cities run by the Chinese central government) – Beijing, Shanghai, Tianjin and Chongqing. There are also five autonomous regions and two special administrative regions – Hong Kong and Macao.

CASE STUDY: HONG KONG AND MACAO

The islands of Hong Kong and Macao on the south coast are China's two special administrative regions (SARs). Hong Kong was ruled by Britain from the 1840s. Following years of pressure from the Chinese government, it was returned to China in 1997, under a special agreement which allowed it to remain largely self-governing. This wealthy island still runs its own economy and has its own currency, but the Chinese government determines matters of foreign policy. This situation was guaranteed for 50 years, until 2047. Macao was taken over by Portugal in 1897. It reverted to China in 1999 under an agreement similar to that made for Hong Kong.

Downtown Hong Kong bristles with tall skyscrapers. Hong Kong is one of the most densely populated places in the world. Lack of space on the island has created a need to construct high-rise buildings.

The five autonomous regions – Inner Mongolia, Guangxi, Xinjiang, Ningxia and Tibet – are home to some of China's largest ethnic minorities, such as Uygurs, Tibetans and Mongols. These regions are not really self-governing, but are mainly ruled by Beijing. China's claim over Tibet (known as Xizang Region) is disputed.

Tibet was an independent state for part of its history, but was taken over by China in 1950. The country's spiritual leader, the Dalai Lama, fled to India in 1959. Many Tibetans would like their country to regain independence. However, since 1989, the Chinese government has actively pursued a policy of resettling Han Chinese in Tibet, where they now outnumber Tibetans.

Limited freedoms

On becoming president in 2003, Hu Jintao pledged to promote good government within China. Yet to date, he has stopped short of

The Potala Palace in Lhasa, Tibet, was the former home of Tibet's spiritual leader, the Dalai Lama, and the seat of the Tibetan government. It is a huge complex of religious and administrative buildings. The palace remains an important pilgrimage site for Tibetan Buddhists.

adopting political reforms that are called for by many Western nations. The Chinese people currently enjoy more freedom than during the early years of Communist rule. However, the government still restricts freedom of speech, workers' rights, and the right to practise religion freely. People who call for political reform, organize workers to argue for better conditions, or criticize the government are liable to be arrested and either imprisoned, exiled (forced to leave China) or executed. The killings in Tiananmen Square in 1989 (see page 15) sent a powerful message to the Chinese people that opposition to the government was not allowed.

FOCUS: CRACKDOWN ON RELIGION

Chinese people are free to practise religion only in approved centres, such as certain temples. In Tibet, monks and nuns who refuse to deny the Dalai Lama are regularly imprisoned. In the 1990s, a spiritual movement based on Buddhist teachings, called the Falun Gong, grew extremely popular in China. In 1999 the government banned the Falun Gong and arrested many of its leaders.

The media and censorship

The Chinese government maintains tight control over the media, including television, radio, newspapers and the Internet. For the first three decades of Communist rule, media such as newspapers and radio were mainly used for political propaganda. Since the 1980s, TV and radio stations have been allowed to broadcast educational programmes and entertainment. The media generally avoids criticism of the government.

Hundreds of newspapers are published in China. Each city has its own newspaper, often supported by local government. China has about one billion television viewers. Radio and television sets are still far more common in cities than in the countryside. Some villages have a communal TV. The government censors all broadcasts and bans broadcasts from foreign TV stations that it believes could threaten China's political stability. By restricting use of satellite dishes, it limits access to foreign news.

Before the 1980s, the telephone system was mainly used by party officials. Now 368 million people have land lines. Use of mobile phones has risen rapidly since 2000. Sending text messages is popular because it is almost impossible for the government to censor information sent by texting.

At the end of 2007, China had more than 170 million Internet users. Internet use is largely confined to cities, which have Internet cafes. The government tries to control the information available to users by blocking sites which discuss banned subjects. Internet cafes that do not follow the strict guidelines are quickly closed down.

China has the world's biggest mobile phone market, with more than 500 million mobile users in 2008.

33

CHAPTER 6

Changing Relationships

China's relations with the outside world have changed considerably in recent decades. Since the 1980s, the need for economic growth has led it to develop closer links with the West.

Relations between superpowers

In the early days of Communism, China's main ally was the Soviet Union. By the late 1950s however, China and the USSR began to draw apart, partly because of differences in foreign policy. In 1960 the USSR stopped sending financial aid to China. Relations between the

US president Richard Nixon during his visit to China in 1972, attending a banquet held in his honour in Shanghai. Chinese premier Zhou Enlai is on his right.

34

two powers remained cool during the following decades, right up until the break-up of the Soviet Union in 1991. Meanwhile, relations with the West, frosty at first, began to thaw. China and the United States established full diplomatic links in the late 1970s, following a historic visit to China by US President Nixon in 1972.

International trade

In 1979, Deng Xiaoping's 'Open Door' policy heralded a new era in international relations, with foreign companies encouraged to invest in China. Before the 1980s, China's main trading partners had been the Soviet Union, Communist countries in eastern Europe, and neighbours such as Japan. Now it began to develop a wider trade network. In 2001 China joined the World Trade Organization, which promotes free trade among its member nations. In 1997, when the island of Hong Kong was returned to China, the country gained a thriving economy and useful business expertise.

Between 2000 and 2005, Chinese exports to the USA rose by over half each year – an astounding achievement. Since then, exports to the USA have continued to rise by 20 per cent each year. China's major trading partners now include the United States, Britain and Germany as well as Asian neighbours. Chief exports include electronic goods, textiles (fabrics), sportswear, transport equipment and foods such as vegetables and tea.

In turn, China's imports have also increased, because it has had to buy in raw materials and technology to develop its industries. Yet the value of China's exports far outweighs its imports. This results in what is called a trade surplus. China's surplus, US $180 billion in 2006, is the largest in the world.

WORLD TRADE

Main exports: Machinery and equipment, plastics, optical and medical equipment, iron and steel
Export partners (2006):
  USA: 21%,
  Hong Kong: 16%,
  Japan: 9.5%,
  South Korea: 4.6%,
  Germany: 4.2%
Main imports: Machinery and equipment, oil and mineral fuels, plastics, optical and medical equipment, organic chemicals, iron and steel
Import partners (2006):
  Japan: 14.6%
  South Korea: 11.3%
  Taiwan: 10.9%
  USA: 7.5%
  Germany: 4.8%
Currency: The yuan, also called the Renminbi (RMB)

Source: CIA World Factbook 2008

International relations

Since the 1980s, China has focused on improving its relations with the outside world. Increased contact has allowed Western nations to put pressure on China to improve its record on human rights and environmental pollution (see Chapter 7). China has also played an increasingly prominent role in international relations. Since 1971, it has been one of five permanent members of the United Nations (UN) Security Council, which promotes peace and stability among nations. The issue of nuclear weapons is always sensitive. Members of the UN Security Council are pledged to limit the number of countries that possess nuclear weapons. When Communist North Korea announced in 2002 that it was developing nuclear weapons, China helped mediate between the UN and its neighbour.

CASE STUDY: TAIWAN

Since 1949 Taiwan has been ruled by Chinese Nationalists who fled China following their defeat by Communist forces (see page 13). Before that, Taiwan had been part of China since the 1680s. The Taiwanese government continues to claim its right to rule China, while the Communists regard Taiwan as a rebellious province and have frequently threatened to invade. In the 1950s and 1960s, Western powers such as the United States acknowledged Taiwan's claim to China. However, in the 1970s, they recognized China's Communist government. Meanwhile, Taiwan's economy grew rapidly in the 1970s, providing China with an example of the advantages of the Western-style economic system.

Rising tourism

China's contact with the outside world has also increased as its tourist industry has expanded. The country is rapidly becoming one of the world's top tourist destinations. In 2000 more than 25 million foreign tourists visited China. By 2006 that figure had grown to 41.8 million. Many visitors come from neighbouring countries such as Japan and Russia, but also from further afield, such as the United States and Europe. China's chief attractions include the Great Wall, the Forbidden City in Beijing, and the tomb of Emperor Qin Shi Huangdi with its army of terracotta warriors.

As China's middle class has grown, so the number of Chinese tourists has also risen rapidly. In 1995–2000, the number of tourists travelling within China more than doubled to 650 million, while in 2006, 34.5 million Chinese travelled abroad.

The tomb of Qin Shi Huangdi near Xi'an is one of China's main tourist attractions. China's first emperor was buried with 7,000 life-size pottery figures of soldiers, designed to protect him in the afterlife. The hidden tomb was accidentally discovered in 1974.

In 2000–07, China prepared for a huge influx of visitors for the 2008 Olympic Games in Beijing. New sports complexes, scores of hotels, and facilities such as shopping malls were built. China also invested heavily to improve its infrastructure, building or upgrading airports, railways and undergrounds.

Emigration

In the 19th and early 20th centuries, the Chinese government severely restricted the number of Chinese allowed to go abroad. Despite this, tens of thousands left China to escape bad treatment or poverty. Chinese emigrants settled all over the world, and now the United States, Canada, Britain, Australia and many other countries have large Chinese communities. One of the effects of emigration is that some features of Chinese culture are now well known internationally – for example Chinese cooking and ancient martial arts.

Chinese emigration is still restricted. This has led to an illegal emigration business. People pay large sums of money to criminal gangs called 'snakeheads' to smuggle them into wealthy countries such as Britain. This illegal activity has led to some tragic incidents. In 2000, 58 Chinese died from suffocation in an airless truck while being smuggled into Britain.

Members of the Chinese community in Sydney, Australia, celebrate the Chinese New Year. This important festival is marked with special food, firecrackers and the famous dragon dance, shown here. Sydney has a large Chinese community; Chinese is the most common second language in the city.

37

CHAPTER 7

Environmental Changes

China is proud of its rich biodiversity – the vast range of plants and animals in different regions around the country. In recent years, however, the country's fast-growing economy and huge population have caused problems for the environment.

Pollution

Many parts of China now suffer from severe air pollution. This is mainly caused by rapid industrialization, with a growing number of factories belching out waste gases. The number of coal- and oil-burning power stations has risen

ANNUAL ENERGY USE AND POLLUTION

Like the USA, China uses a vast amount of energy, but it uses far less energy per person than the USA.

	China	USA
Total energy consumption (in 1,000s of tonnes, 2003)	1,381,297	2,280,881
World ranking in total fossil fuel consumption	2	1
Energy consumption per person in kg	1,138	7,795
Total CO_2 emissions in tonnes (2003)	3,958	5,720
CO_2 emissions per person (2002)	2.9	19.9
Number of vehicles per 1,000 people (2002)	12.4	779.4

Source: World Resources Institute, 2008

quickly to meet the rocketing demand for energy from industry and cities. The dramatic rise in vehicles has also contributed to air pollution. The air in many of China's cities is highly polluted, which causes breathing problems for many citizens. Some of China's cities, including Beijing, rank among the most polluted cities in the world.

Air pollution makes the rain that falls in many parts of China slightly acidic. When acid rain drains away into rivers and wetlands, it harms plants and animals. China's rivers and lakes are also polluted by chemicals from farms and factories, and by sewage from cities. Less than 15 per cent of China's waste water is treated; the rest remains polluted, and can cause illness among people and wildlife. In addition, land pollution is a problem, particularly in mining regions, where huge heaps of waste rock build up around the mines.

(Opposite) **China's rising consumption of fossil fuels (coal, oil and natural gas) is making a significant contribution to world emissions of carbon dioxide – one of the chief gases that is causing global warming.**

China's government is under growing pressure to 'clean up its act'. In 2003 it pledged to improve air quality in cities, and is planning to increase its use of renewable energies such as wind, water, and solar power (energy from the sun). Renewable energy sources do not cause pollution, but large-scale schemes such as hydroelectric plants impact on the environment (see pages 21–22). To reduce air pollution caused by vehicles, the government is encouraging people to return to using bicycles to travel to work or school. Recycling is also being encouraged throughout China.

Habitat loss

China's plants and animals are also coming under increasing pressure from human development. China's varied habitats – natural places where plants and animals live – include grasslands, wetlands, mountains and tropical, broad-leaved and conifer forests. Parts of these habitats have been damaged. For example, large areas of wetlands have been drained to create new land for farms or towns. River habitats have been altered by engineering projects such as canals and dams.

About 11 per cent of China is covered by forest. Over the last few decades, large areas of forest have been felled for timber or fuel, or to create land to build on. Deforestation leads to soil erosion on the bare hillsides, while the soil that drains away into rivers increases the risk of flooding.

Parts of China's grasslands are suffering from overgrazing (allowing animals to graze too much in one area). This results in erosion and is causing China's deserts to expand – a problem called desertification. Together, erosion and construction are believed to have caused the loss of about one-fifth of China's farmland since 1950. The Chinese government is aware of the scale of habitat loss, deforestation and desertification, and is taking steps to tackle these problems. For example, it has greatly reduced its tree-felling programme, and as a result, has had to buy in timber from abroad.

Forest and resort houses on the Hulun Buir grassland of Inner Mongolia Autonomous Region in north-east China. The grasslands are suffering from desertification because of overgrazing.

In 2001 China launched a massive tree-planting programme; by 2006, more than 12 billion trees had been planted. To combat desertification, it is creating a belt of forest 4,500 km long.

Endangered species

China's diverse wildlife includes 32,000 plants, 400 mammals and 1,200 birds. Within this variety are many unique species, such as the giant panda, Yangtze dolphin and Yangtze alligator. Unfortunately, habitat loss, development and hunting have made some species scarce. The survival of the extremely rare Yangtze dolphin and Yangtze alligator is threatened by the

Three Gorges Dam, which has greatly reduced the river water. The snow leopard and Manchurian tiger have been hunted close to extinction. Endangered species such as these are now protected by law, but are still killed by poachers (people who hunt illegally).

Chinese conservationists believe that the best way of preserving rare animals is to protect the habitat where they live. China has 1,270 parks and nature reserves, covering 12 per cent of its land area, and more are planned, to cover 16 per

cent of China by 2010. Endangered species such as the giant panda are now found mainly in reserves. Rare species are also bred in captivity, with the aim of releasing young animals into the wild.

FOCUS: THE ENDANGERED SNOW LEOPARD

The snow leopard inhabits the rugged mountains of Tibet. This powerful cat preys on wild sheep and goats. The snow leopard's spotted coat provides perfect camouflage, but also makes it a target for fur-hunters. The animal's bones are ground up and used in traditional Chinese medicine, although this is illegal. Conservationists estimate that fewer than 2,000 of these magnificent cats are left in China. They are on the list of protected species, and parts of their habitat have been made into nature reserves.

A fierce predator, the snow leopard follows its prey – wild sheep and goats – as they move up to the high mountain pastures in summer, and down to sheltered valleys for the winter.

CHAPTER 8

Future Challenges

Change once happened very slowly in China. In the past few decades it has come incredibly quickly, as China has become a leading player in the world economy. Many experts predict the 21st century will be China's century. It certainly began well for China, with the country launching its manned space programme in 2003 – only the third country to do so, after the USSR and the United States. In 2008 it further raised its world profile by hosting the Olympic Games.

In 2007 many old districts of Beijing were demolished to build sports stadiums like this one for the Olympic Games. Many residents complained that they did not receive enough compensation for losing their homes.

A grandfather holds his sole grandchild – a product of China's One-Child Policy. In 2007 it was announced the policy would remain in place. Yet a special rule allows couples formed of two people with no brothers or sisters to have two children.

Economy

In the next few years, China will overtake the United States as the world's largest economy. Many Western nations that invested in China in the 1980s are now looking to China to return the favour, and invest in their own industries. One of the key challenges will be to sustain economic growth without sacrificing the environment. China plans its economy in five-year periods. The 11th Five-Year Plan, for 2006–11, calls for an ambitious 45 per cent increase in China's GDP by 2010, while making a 20 per cent reduction in energy use. The plan states the importance of conserving the environment, but lacks detail as to how this will be achieved.

Social concerns

China's economic success has brought prosperity for some, but also growing unrest and new social problems. It has led to a widening gulf between city and country, and between the new middle class and millions of poor rural workers. Unemployment has risen steeply as state-owned industries have closed. All China's people share a common desire for higher living standards, but since these increase energy use, they come at a cost to the environment.

In 2003 the new president Hu Jintao pledged to build a 'harmonious society' and close the gap

FOCUS: AN AGEING POPULATION

The size of China's population remains a key concern. In the near future, China will face the consequences of its One-Child Policy – a fast-ageing population. As healthcare has improved, so people are living longer. Around 2020, huge numbers of people will reach retirement age, with a dwindling working population earning money to support them. The government is likely to face pressure to relax its One-Child Policy. Yet it must avoid a rapid population rise, which would undermine its ability to feed its people.

between rich and poor by improving health and education in rural areas. He also pledged to fight corruption, which is common at all levels of society. Whether rich or poor, there is a growing will among Chinese people for increased freedom. However, the government has shown little sign of allowing its citizens greater freedom and improving its record on human rights. To remain popular, it needs to ensure that more of its vast population share in its new-found wealth.

Timeline

1766 BCE Shang dynasty is founded
1122 BCE Zhou dynasty is founded
551–479 BCE Life of the philosopher Confucius
221 BCE Shi Huangdi becomes China's first emperor
206 BCE Han rulers take over from the Qin dynasty
c. 100 CE Buddhism reaches China
220–581 CE Period of unrest, during which China is split into three kingdoms
581 Sui dynasty reunifies China
618 Tang dynasty begins
907–960 Time of unrest, called the Second Intermediate Period
960 Song dynasty begins
1252–79 Mongol emperor Kublai Khan conquers China
1368 The Ming dynasty takes over
1644 Rule by Ch'ing emperors from Manchuria begins
1839–42 First Opium War
1856–60 Second Opium War
1894–5 China is defeated in a war with Japan
1898–1900 Boxer Uprising: Chinese secret societies rebel against foreign influence in China
1911 China's last emperor is deposed
1912 The Nationalists declare China a republic

1927 Civil war between Nationalists and Communists
1931 Japan invades northern China
1937–45 War with Japan, which invades China during World War II
1945 Japan is defeated. Fighting resumes between Nationalists and Communists
1949 Communists proclaim the People's Republic of China
1950 China and the Soviet Union become allies. China occupies Tibet
1958 Chairman Mao announces the Great Leap Forward
1960 The Soviet Union stops aid to China
1966 Mao launches the Cultural Revolution
1978 Reformer Deng Xiaoping becomes president
1989 The Chinese government puts down pro-democracy demonstrations
1997 Deng Xiaoping dies. Britain returns Hong Kong to China
2001 China joins the World Trade Organization
2003 China sends its first astronaut into space
2006 Work on the Three Gorges Dam is essentially completed
2008 The Olympic Games are held in Beijing

Glossary

acid rain Rain that is slightly acidic because it is polluted by waste gases.
autonomous Self-governing.
basin The area drained by a river and its streams.
censorship When a state or organization controls information and may prevent it from being published or broadcast.
civil service The government departments and officials that run a country.
Communist Ruled like the system of government in the Soviet Union, where the government owned and controlled the means of production, such as farms and mines.
conservationists People who work to protect wild habitats and their plants and animals.

constitution A set of laws governing a country or organization.
deforestation Cutting down so many trees that forests cannot grow back.
democracy A political system in which people vote for their rulers in free elections.
depose To overthrow a ruler.
desertification When the size of a desert increases, often due to erosion.
dynasty A series of rulers of a country from the same family.
emigration Moving to live permanently in another country.
emission When a substance such as a gas is released.

ethnic minority A group of people who have a different culture, religion, language or skin colour from most other people in their society.

export To sell goods to another country.

fossil fuel A fuel made from the fossilized remains of plants or animals, such as coal, oil and natural gas.

free trade A system under which private companies can trade without government involvement.

global warming A worldwide rise in temperatures, caused by air pollution.

Gross Domestic Product (GDP) The total value of all goods and services produced by a country in a year.

hydroelectricity Electricity that is produced using the power of fast-flowing water.

imperial Of or belonging to an emperor.

imports Goods from another country.

industrialization When a country develops factories to produce goods.

infrastructure The facilities needed for a country to function well, including power supplies, communication and transport.

manufacturing The making of products.

market The amount of business in a particular area.

middle class The people in society who are neither very rich nor poor.

migration When people or animals move from one place to another.

Nationalist Someone who is committed to the independence of his or her country.

raw materials Materials that are used to make other products.

real growth rate The rate of change in GDP from one year to the next.

renewable energy Energy that comes from sources such as wind, sun and waves, and will not run out.

republic A state without a king or queen.

revolutionary Of the forces that rise against a country's government or ruler.

soil erosion The wearing away of the land through natural processes or through activities such as mining or the grazing of animals.

tundra The barren treeless lowlands of the north, where the temperature is low all year round.

Further information

Books

Changing Face of China by Stephen Keeler (Hodder Wayland, 2007)

China by Ali Brownlie Bojang and Nicola Barber (Hodder Wayland, 2006)

China by Jen Green (National Geographic Society, 2006)

DK Eyewitness Travel Guides: China (Dorling Kindersley, 2005)

Nations of the World: China by Catherine Field (Raintree, 2004)

River Journeys: The Yangtze by Rob Bowden (Hodder Wayland, 2005)

Websites

en.wikipedia.org/wiki/China Wikipedia

news.bbc.co.uk/1/hi/in_depth/asia_pacific/2004/china/default.stm BBC reports on China

news.bbc.co.uk/1/hi/world/asia-pacific/country_profiles/1287798.stm BBC country profile

www.china.org.cn/english/index.htm China.org: China's official news and information site

www.cia.gov/library/publications/the-world-factbook/geos/ch.html CIA (US Central Intelligence Agency) World Factbook

Index